Letters from the Soul

Letters from the Soul

Unsent Letters and Stories
for Spiritual Growth

Rose Offner

GIBBS·SMITH
P
PUBLISHER

Salt Lake City

First Edition
00 99 98 97   5 4 3 2 1

This is a Peregrine Smith Book
published by
Gibbs Smith, Publisher
P.O. Box 667
Layton, Utah 84041
For orders only: 800-748-5439

Photographs of shrines in Italy contributed by Tom Hubbard
Photograph of woman crying by Debora Cartwright

Printed in Hong Kong

ISBN 0-87905-793-9

To God, who sends me love and strength.

*To my mom, Johnie Ruiz, for helping to make
my dreams possible.*

*In loving memory of my grandma, Rose Bevona,
who is greatly missed.*

Acknowledgments

A heartfelt thanks to all those who generously shared their letters and were willing to tell their stories. Your contributions added a richness to this book and made it a gift of inspiration and love. Thanks to Mike Miller, Linda Rolph, Anne Taddei.

Everyone who touched this book blessed it. I wish to thank:

Gibbs Smith, my publisher, for holding the vision and giving me the opportunity and tools to make it a special gift.

Linda Mead, agent extraordinaire, for professional skills, talents, assistance with the manuscript, and the gift of time when I was in need.

Madge Baird for editorial guidance.

Christopher Robbins, Rosalind Willey, Sue Carabine and the Gibbs Smith team for all the hard work you do; I appreciate you all.

Debora Cartwright for the beautiful photo of the woman crying. Tom Hubbard for permission to use the photos of the shrines in Italy.

Trudy Totty for friendship, support and working hand in hand to bring this together.

Judy Davis, Lois Arigotti, Marie Davies, and Marcelle Heath for assistance with the manuscript. I also want to thank those who took their valuable time to listen to me read stories or letters and gave me feedback: Sandra at Full Circle Books; Willie Hooks, author; and Jack Newton.

The book stores that have supported my work. I am especially grateful to Kathy Scheer at A Clean Well-Lighted Place for Books and Catherine Barcos at Book Passage.

A loving thanks to my family: my daughter, Danielle Offner; my mom, Johnie Ruiz; Rich Srsen; Robert Ruiz; Aaron and Gina Ruiz; Beverlee and Paul Gillmore and family; Mike and Vicki Vargo; Trish Smith; Rand Smith. I love you all.

A heartfelt thanks to my friends who helped me through hard times: Anne Taddei, Wendy and Barry McLaughlin, Debi Fernandez, Lois Arigotti, Michael Fogli, Colleen Holden, Wendy and Tom Hubbard.

CONTENTS

About
Letters from the Soul
and the Power of the Unsent Letter

The private nature of letter writing allows us a view into the heart and soul. *Letters from the Soul* is a book of unsent letters and true stories. It gives us evidence of the power of the unsent letter and the written word. The letters were written by people who are on a spiritual path. They were willing to invest the time and do the work it takes to forgive, heal, and love.

Unsent letters are letters we write and never send. Unsent letters work because they help us to voice our feelings. We write them to get our feelings out, to express ourselves from the heart. Writing unsent letters has empowered people who have taken my workshops to heal their past, create their dreams and find the sacredness in their journey. Unsent letters make conscious what may have been unconscious. Because the letters don't get sent, we don't have to censor them. We can rage, get as angry as we want, express

9

ourselves truthfully, no holds barred. Letter writing is a form of journaling.

Unsent letters help us find answers because our words and intentions create a momentum in the universe. We know our letters have been answered when we receive a solution to a challenge, an intuitive flash, a feeling of resolution.

Tears often come when we write unsent letters. Our tears create an opening in the heart. They often signify a healing. This is another way we know our unsent letters have been received.

Unsent letters can be written to God, your father, your mother, the higher power of those you love and those with whom you have unfinished business. You can even write letters to those who have passed away. Writing imaginary letters gives us a vehicle for hearing the things we wanted to hear but never heard.

10

This book describes four distinctive types of unsent letters, though many more can develop from these. All are powerful:

Inner child letters allow us to release childhood wounds, express feelings and thoughts we have buried, and heal ourselves and our relationships.

Spiritual correspondence are letters written to God, guardian angels, our higher self, or whatever name one gives to the Spirit of Life—written in times of need and times of joy to express our deepest fears and our gratitudes. When we listen for the answers, God or Life itself responds.

Letters to life's teachers are written to the fears, problems, barriers, and other circumstances that occur in our lives. As we write, surprising insights unfold that help us see and resolve the issues we are facing.

Correspondence with others are letters that express things we wanted to say but didn't, or words we wanted to hear from someone else but didn't. These letters can also be used to resolve our feelings that result from the death of loved ones, estrangements, or other types of partings.

I have been teaching self-esteem, personal-growth, and weight-loss classes for over ten years now. Knowing the power of journal keeping, I ask all my students to keep journals. The results are phenomenal, from increased self-love and peaceful divorces to overcoming obsessive relationships, healing relationships with parents, and losing weight by doing the inner work of dealing with addiction or resistance and creating our dreams and desires.

Our letters and journals chronicle our lives. Writing unsent letters and keeping a journal saved my life. I was able to overcome a drug addiction, leave an unhealthy relationship, and fulfill my life's dreams.

It is my hope that you will be inspired to write your own unsent letters and stories. When life challenges you and gives you more than you can bear, that is the time to start writing. You can also write when you have gratitude and love to express.

This book has a special section at the end of each chapter for you to make your own unsent letters and stories, complete with artfully designed pages and envelopes where you can open your heart to healing and love.

Inner Child Letters

We all have an "inner child." When we allow the child in us to speak, we can release childhood hurts, express feelings and thoughts we have buried, and heal ourselves and our relationships.

When writing inner child letters, use a crayon or pencil in your nondominant hand (i.e., left hand if you are right-handed and vice versa). And write on ruled newsprint paper like you used in first grade. As you write on those thick, light blue lines and see your printing develop a bit of a scribble, memories and feelings you had when you were a child come back.

Writing inner child letters allows us to speak from that place within where we are frightened or overwhelmed. As you write from that tender place that was hurt, old childhood issues that are longing to be healed surface. It also gives us the opportunity to address the child that still lives inside of us.

I have conducted this writing exercise with rooms full of people—men and women alike—and there have been times when there was not a dry eye in the room. This process is very evocative, so keep tissues in hand and welcome your tears—they are a gift. They help us to wash away our hurts and to heal our hearts.

Dear Dad,

I don't feel like you know me. We never played together. I always wanted to play. I don't feel like we are close. I want to know if you feel close to me. You made me feel bad a lot. I would like to become friends. Let's talk. I love you. I hope you love me.

Love,
Mike

Mike's Story

Dumping anything onto a sheet of paper is always good. It wasn't that the letters I wrote contained any new information, but they were a part of my whole recovery process.

Being gay and not being able to talk about my life or my partner kept me feeling isolated from my family. In recovery we're taught that we are as sick as our secrets; our secrets are the worst things we can have. I really didn't even want to go back home for a long time because I didn't feel like I could be myself and talk about my life. It took a while before I finally told my family I was gay and a while longer before I told my dad.

The letter was a continuation of ongoing therapy that helped me get out of the father-son role and work on my relationship with my father. I don't play that little-boy role anymore.

My dad is a big factor in my life. But now, instead of feeling anxious about our relationship, I feel sorry for him. He's been so busy raising a family that he really hasn't had time for himself.

In my family, if you wanted to talk to my dad, you did it through my mom. She would say, "Don't talk to him now—wait until after he eats," or, "Don't ask him now, he's in a bad mood." So he ended up being excluded from certain things in the family. But I couldn't really see that till now. It's almost like he got typecast as being the bad guy and we all just believed it.

For a long time, I wanted to tell my dad I was gay, but my family didn't think it was a good idea. They weren't sure about how my dad would react, and they were worried. My dad and I have had a long history of noncommunication or surface communication only. Finally, I decided to do what was right for me.

I had gone home for a visit and we were both up early one morning. It was a rare opportunity. Out came the words, "Dad, I'm gay." I didn't know what to expect. He looked at me and then hugged me and said, "It doesn't matter. I love you anyway."

Recently I asked my family what they thought about my bringing my partner home for our family reunion. My dad surprised everyone and said it would be fine. So, we are going home. In fact, my partner's family is having their reunion also, so we're going to both.

Author's note:
I could hardly wait to hear how it went and thought you might want to know too. Both families were totally supportive, and the people whom Mike had anticipated the worst from were great. There was no drama. In fact, Mike's partner's parents went so far as to write and call him in advance to welcome him.

Spiritual Correspondence

We can write letters to God, our Guardian Angels, our higher self, or whatever name we give to the Spirit of Life or our Creator. These letters are best described as written prayers. When we listen for the answer, God or Life itself responds.

Writing letters to or from God is also a way of verbalizing the prayers and gratitude that we have. Spiritual correspondence is a way of reaching the divine, a way of making special requests from God for assistance in reaching goals and achieving our heart's desires.

Our higher self is the spiritual part of us, the part that is able to rise above our self-doubt and even our anger. Our higher self can look at our situations with love and compassion. Writing to our higher self allows us to increase in self-love.

Writing higher-self letters also gives us a way to request help for ourselves and those we are concerned about. These letters also help us to become aware of and tap into the higher qualities of our own soul—qualities such as peace, strength,

patience, forgiveness, or whatever qualities we may need
at the time.

We can also correspond with angels by writing them letters.
Of course, this isn't the only way we can communicate with
them, but it is one way to have tangible evidence of divine
communication. Angel letters are an effective way for us to
send a written prayer on behalf of someone we would like
to be watched over. They can also help us to take life lightly.
Angel letters work because our words have power, and writing
or speaking these words gives clarity to our thoughts, desires
and intentions.

The answers come. All we need to do is listen from that quiet
place in our hearts. We can receive answers through our intu-
itions. Answers also show up through synchronized events.
Answers enter our thoughts as we sit down with a pen and
paper and allow ourselves to receive what comes with an open
heart. The heavens conspire to support us. Suddenly doors
open, and that which we need or desire begins to arrive.

To the Guardian Angel of My Runaway Daughter

I know you have guided my daughter this far in her life and have protected her and guided her to love. Please assist her now in her time of need and apparent confusion. Give her the strength to say no to wrong choices and yes to the right ones.

Remind her that as her mother I am always there for her, and that no matter what she does, my love and support will endure throughout. Fill her thoughts with clarity, and gently pave the way for her safe and longed-for return. Allow those whom she comes in contact with to remind her of the love that is inside of her, the love that surrounds her. Please remind her that running away is never the answer in life, and that no matter where you run, you can never escape yourself.

Please protect her and keep her safe from harm's way. Assist her on her journey to adulthood; ease the struggles, challenges and confusion she bears. Fill her with love for herself, and remind her of her family's love and care.

Thank you for always watching over my beautiful child.

In gratitude,
Her Mother

A Mother's Story

When my daughter became a teenager, she changed.
Overnight my angel turned into the teenage demon from hell.
She started cutting school, lying, and had an attitude.

One day we had a terrible fight—one of the many we had been
having. I don't remember what it was about, but it started with
some arguing and then progressed to yelling and my telling
her to go to her room. She glared at me defiantly and then said
"no." She had never said no before. I felt like hitting her and
wrestling her to the floor. My feelings really surprised me
since I didn't believe in spanking or hitting.

She finally went to her room. Twenty minutes later, I had a
feeling that something was wrong. I knocked on her bedroom
door, turned the knob and went in. The curtains were blowing
in the breeze and a rap song was playing on the radio. She
was gone.

I was furious and scared. How could she be so bold? My
daughter was like a stranger to me in every way. I didn't know

what to expect anymore. Everything she was doing was so unlike her. I ran to my car and drove around looking for her. When I couldn't find her, I started calling her friends.

I stared out the front window all night, wondering where she was and worrying about her. I even left her window open so she could sneak back in if she wanted.

The phone rang and I jumped. It was her dad saying someone had seen her in the town nearby. A truck pulled up in front of my house. It was my uncle. He had come to help me find her. "Don't worry," he said. "I asked my guardian angel to help us find her." We drove to the area where she had been seen and somehow ended up at the bus station. I jumped out of the truck and ran to the station attendant and showed him her picture. "Oh, yeah," he said, "she was just here asking how to get to Half Moon Bay. Wait here and I'll see if I can find her." Moments later, she was walking toward us.

I wish I could say that was my last sleepless night. But the truth is, it was the beginning of her running away and taking night escapades.

The consequences I gave her were hard on both of us. Since I had to be there to reinforce them, it felt like I was being punished too.

The tension had been mounting. We were both pacing the house and having another argument. She was standing in front of my face only inches away, posturing. I suddenly had this idea and said, "So, you seem like you want to fight."

"Yeah," she said.

"Okay, let's move the furniture out of the way. We'll have a wrestling match. Whoever gets pinned two out of three times wins." We established the rules and began. Within minutes we were both laughing. She won, but I felt like I had won too. We both felt better.

The next time she took off, I sat down after hours of agonizing and wrote her guardian angel a letter. Within an hour of the writing, she was home. That was the last time she ran away.

When we sat down to have our heart-to-heart, I said, "You know, honey, you haven't been very good lately. But the truth is, I haven't been there for you. I've been working way too much lately and haven't given you the time or attention you need and deserve. I'm really sorry, sweetie, and I'm going to try harder. Will you too?"

"Yeah, Mom. I really will. I'm not cutting school anymore, and I am trying."

We have both tried, and although things still aren't perfect, we're making strides in the right direction and improvements are visible.

It has taken me quite a while to recover from all the "drama," as she calls it. For months, I would wake up two or three times a night and check on her to make sure she was still there. And early one morning when I heard a car door slam and tires screeching around the corner, I jumped out of bed and found myself chasing a car, running in my pajamas, racing as fast as I could—only to realize it was the newspaper boy.

Letter to My Husband's Higher Self

During this time of change, please make my husband aware of your presence through love and confidence. Help his heart to understand and accept the changes in his life. Let him know he is loved, and allow him to open his heart and feel worthy of love. Help him to know that I have not abandoned him, even though we will not be living together under the

same roof. Help him to allow his friends to give their strength and support.

Keep him strong in mind and body and spirit. Nurture and nourish him mentally, physically, and spiritually. Help him to clearly see the paths before him, and help him to choose wisely.

Bring him peace of mind. Comfort him and love him.

Amen.

Letter to My Higher Self

My husband finally voiced today what I've been thinking for weeks. He wants to know my plans. So do I. Throughout this whole process, I've not panicked—at least not since I made my final decision to leave. I've been comfortable in my decision and have felt that all things would fall into place in their own time. This included finding an apartment. Please help me to remain calm and focused as this separation moves to fruition. Help me to find motivation as I search for a new home. Give me strength to

deal with the day-to-day frustrations
and challenges I face as I move toward my
new life. Help me to remember that I
love myself and am making this move
for me—for my growth as a
spirit and hopefully as a person.

Help me to be sensitive and
understanding toward my
husband and his feelings.

Finally, help me to find that
special place to live that will
be a haven and comfortable
place in which to grow
spiritually. Let me recognize
it and move forward
without doubts and
reservations. Help me to
trust in myself and my decisions.

Send me love.
Linda

Linda's Story

Choosing to separate is a difficult decision. My husband was asking me what my plans were. Yet I really didn't know. It wasn't clear until I wrote the letters.

My husband was having a difficult time while I was making my decision, and I was worried about him. One night he was having such a hard time that he got up and went outside.

That's when I started writing. Writing the letters helped me to feel comfortable with my decision to leave the marriage. And it helped to alleviate the doubt that creeps in. After I wrote the letters, I knew it was the right decision.

When my husband came back inside that night, he couldn't relax. So I read the letters to him. After I read them, we both

felt better; it was a relief. It helped him to let me go and reminded him that he is loved. They helped me to be understanding and to remain sensitive to his feelings.

I was reminded that I was making the move for my growth as a spirit and a person. Even though it's not what I really wanted, I knew it was for the best.

I knew my letters were answered. I found a comfortable place to live. It's the haven I was looking for. And my husband was invited on a trip to Europe; his friends were giving him their support.

Time has passed and my husband and I remain friends. There are peaceful ways of separating.

A place for your own Spiritual Correspondence and Stories

Write a Spiritual Correspondence letter and place it in an envelope you create and glue here.

Letters to Life's Teachers

Some of our greatest teachers in life are the fears, problems, barriers, and other circumstances that occur. We learn some of our greatest lessons through our interactions with these teachers. We can dialogue with them through unsent letters. When we name them and ask, "Why are you in my life?" we gain surprising insights and come to see what we can do to resolve our current challenges in life.

Where are you currently stuck in your life? What is your most consuming problem? After you have identified it, write it a letter. The "it" I am talking about is your anger, stress, resistance, loneliness, or any other emotion or problem. As we face our fears, we come to recognize them as sacred allies on our journey. We begin self-exploration by asking questions. The questions we ask of Life are more important than the answers. As we listen for answers and write the responses we receive without judging our thoughts, Soul becomes our guide.

Letter to Loneliness

Dear Loneliness,

He is gone now, and all I've done is cry. I can barely handle this terrible ache in my chest. You are the hurt that overwhelms me, the feelings I can barely express. Every time the phone rings, I pray it's him. And I dread it will be him. If it isn't him, you make my heart sink; if it is him, you make my heart freeze. You are the longing. You are the void I am feeling, the sadness that is consuming me. I know you are here to teach me something, and that these feelings are the part of love that cannot be avoided. When I think of him now, I wonder if it's him that I miss or the idea of him.

Me

Story of Loneliness

Love is what I've always wanted—well, love, friendship and companionship. Yet at night we slept on opposite ends of the bed on cold, crisp sheets and tried hard not to touch. If we happened to touch, we would quickly pull away. In the center of the bed was a vast wasteland that we didn't dare enter, and if we did it was only in our sleep and then only by accident.

There were years when I was lonely, though not because I was alone. In fact, I was in a relationship at the time. But being together in a loveless way and living with invisible barriers that were built for protection was hard. In time the walls became real. At night I cried as quietly as I could. They were big, silent tears that formed a salty pool on my pillow. Even when we spent time together, I was filled with a crushing loneliness that consumed me.

Loneliness is tangible when you're in a relationship that isn't working.

Finally he left. Though there were days when loneliness would still visit, it was no longer with me every day. The truth is, I was far less lonely without him than I was when we were together.

At first I wanted to blame him, as though someone were to blame. But then I came to see that he didn't do anything to me; everything that happened I allowed. I was not a victim but a participant.

I remembered hearing a psychic on the radio say, "Whenever you're rejected, you are being protected." I knew in my heart of hearts that somehow it was true I was being protected from something, although at the time I didn't know what it was. I know now, and I am glad we're not together.

Now I see that being in or out of a relationship isn't what brings up feelings of loneliness, and a relationship doesn't automatically fulfill the need for love. That depends on the relationship itself and on your feelings about yourself. I can see now that you can be alone and still not feel lonely if you are comfortable with yourself.

Whenever I get sad and start to miss him, I quickly remind myself that it was the *idea* of him that I missed and not him.

A place for your own Letters to Life's Teachers and Stories

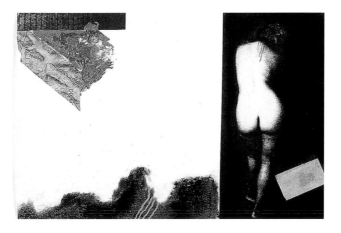

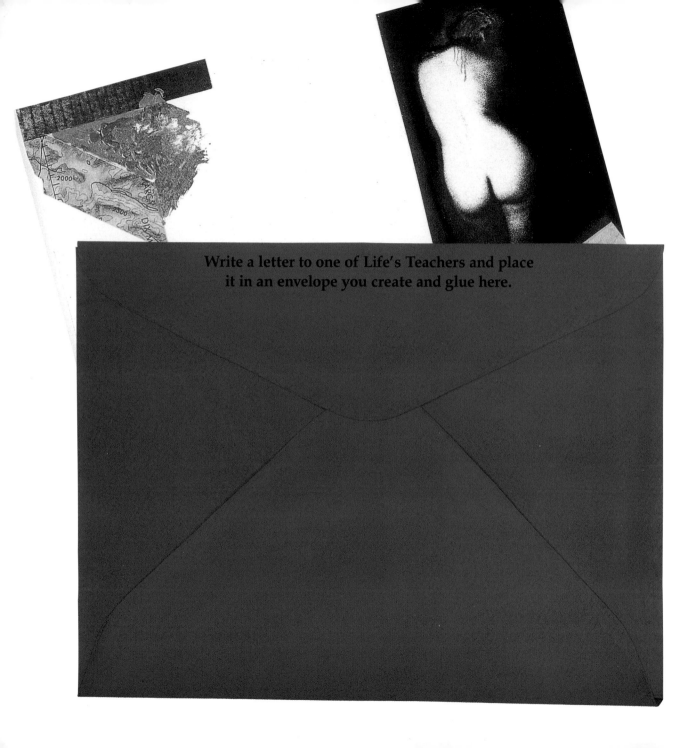

Write a letter to one of Life's Teachers and place
it in an envelope you create and glue here.

Correspondence with Others

Correspondence with others allows us to express things we wanted to say but didn't, or words we wanted to hear from someone else but didn't. We do not need to send the letter. The power of the unsent letter is not in the sending but in the expressing of what is in our hearts.

Imagined letters are an important part of our correspondence with others. These are letters we write to ourselves from someone else, saying things we wish they would have said. They work especially well for unresolved issues with our parents or any relationship that we feel needs closure or healing. We can correspond with others to express our unresolved anger or love. It is a way for us to express the inexpressible.

If the person is deceased, we can still write to them or imagine they write to us. And when we speak our truth from the heart and then write the response we want to hear, tears may come. When they do, we have reached that place of compassion where we are understood and where we understand; that place where there is an absence of judgment or recrimination; that place which the poet Rumi describes as "the field beyond right doing and wrong doing." This is the meeting ground where we are united in soul and we begin to heal ourselves and our relationships.

An imagined
Letter from My Mom

My dearest Anne,

My dear, dear child, I sure miss you. You were always so
very special to me.

Thank you for taking care of Lisa. I know it was difficult
and that you did the best you could. I will always be grateful
to you for that.

Heaven isn't what you think. It's much, much more. I wish
there were words to describe it. But the spoken word has never
been able to quite capture the spiritual. Don't let your thirst

for spirituality ever be quenched. It is through the yearning that you find the answers.

I know you have struggled. I've been there beside you along the way, and my heart went out to you. I am so glad you felt my presence. I was afraid you wouldn't.

We are so much alike, you know. I guess that's why we are such kindred spirits.

The journey is shorter than you think, hon. Keep your eyes focused, your heart open, and your soul prepared. And when you round the bend, one of the first things you will see is me running toward you with my face beaming and my arms outstretched.

My love always,
Mom

Anne's Story

I was at a workshop when I wrote this letter. Yet it wasn't a letter that I sat down to write; in fact, I was planning on writing a letter to my kids. What came out was this letter from my mother, who died seventeen years ago.

I'm a very private person. So I was surprised when I was sitting there in this workshop with tears running down my face, sobbing. But I kept myself writing through the tears, even though I could barely see through the blur. It was interesting because it wasn't as though I had any unfinished business with my mom. In fact, I remember thinking while I was writing that I didn't have any unresolved issues. Yet it's had a powerful effect on me. I still can't read it without crying.

It affected my sisters the same way when I shared it with them. It was so clearly my mom speaking through me—her words, her tone, her spirit.

Now, whenever I hear of someone I know who has lost a loved one, I tell them I know that our loved ones still hear us and are always with us, even after death. And they still feel our pain.

It felt like my mom was saying she wanted me to know that she is still with me.

It's comforting to know that after I die I will still be there for my kids. I always knew there was life after, but this confirmed it for me. And those times that I felt my mom's presence, she really was there. The power of the letter is that it gives those we love a chance to say things they need to say. It gives those we love a voice.

to My Father

A Daughter's Story

"Hey, stupid," he said. Then the loud slap of his hand would ring inside of my head, and my eyes would turn down to the floor where I would stare. No one can touch my head today, unless it's done respectfully.

My uncle didn't know that. We were just getting ready to sit down to Thanksgiving dinner—everyone was laughing and having fun—when my uncle jokingly hit me the same way my dad used to before he would yell "stupid."

I stood there, shocked. Immediately the memories were there, flooding back to me. It wasn't my uncle who was hitting me, but my dad. I could still feel the slap of his hand, and then it seemed as though I could hear that ringing sound that always followed.

But this time, instead of putting my head down in shame, I came back from the journey of that memory and responded with such vehemence that it stopped everything and everyone. Suddenly, from somewhere deep inside, the little girl that is still alive inside of me had a voice and it was big and loud. It shocked even me.

"Don't you ever touch me like that again. My dad hit me like that, and I don't think it's funny."

"I'm sorry," he said. He was still shocked at my strong reaction. I guess we all were. We all sat down to eat, stunned and a little uncomfortable.

Finally, I realized just how deeply my father's words had affected me. For all those years, I had suffered with the conscious and unconscious belief that I was stupid. I realized my father was wrong. He had made a terrible mistake. I decided to forgive him for both of us, and that's what led me to write the letter.

After I wrote the letter, I had the courage to say these things to my dad. We both cried. I could tell he was grateful. He died suddenly two weeks later. I make jokes now about how it saved me thousands of dollars in therapy, although I believe that's true.

A place for your own Correspondence with Others and Stories

Rose Offner, a motivational speaker and writer, is the author of *Journal to the Soul*, an illuminated book of guided processes for sacred journal keeping. Her Journal to the Soul workshops are regularly attended events that have helped hundreds of people find the sacredness in life's journey. Ms. Offner lives in the San Francisco Bay Area with her daughter, Danielle.

For information regarding Rose Offner's books, tapes, lectures, workshops, and consulting arrangements, contact:

From the Inside Out
2030 Pioneer Ct.
San Mateo, CA 94403
(415) 571-6251